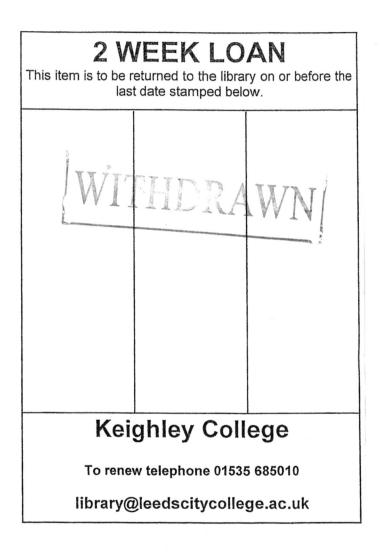

Mattock

Plasters Float

Lump Hammer

Cold Chisel

Peg

the perfect
P O N D
recipe book

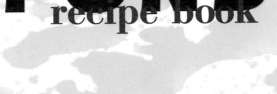

Published by Kingdom Books
PO Box 15
Waterlooville PO7 6BQ
England

Desiged By Add Graphics
PO Box 15
Waterlooville P07 6BQ
England

Spade

Shovel

Trowel

Hose

Cement

Wheel Barrow

Level

CONTENTS

the perfect
POND
recipe book

by
Peter J May

KINGDOM

GB-002

To have the sight and sound of water near them in a garden has been an almost instinctive urge to people of all cultures in all ages. Apart from the importance of water for the sustenance of life, in ancient times an area of water had important religious significance. It was a place where gods lounged and frolicked and nymphs bathed. To other cultures in different times water and its control became a symbol of power and wealth.

Now as then, the beauty of reflection, the relaxing sound of moving water and the life that it attracts make the water garden as desirable to many people as a lawn or patio. However people also see that creating a water garden can be a very expensive project. As the Garden Centres' shelves groan with an ever-increasing array of water garden products, the newcomer to this area of gardening may also be daunted by the choice of products and materials.

Another problem might be that the creation of a water garden seems far beyond the novices' practical or physical skills. Those that do take the plunge often do so armed with a brilliant idea but a limited grasp of potential problems and little knowledge of the possibilities that existing materials can provide.

This book aims to provide you with the information necessary to create the water garden of your dreams. It will help you see not only the limitations but also the possibilities of your ideas and will help you to avoid the pitfalls at each stage of construction. It will save you the heartache of seeing the results of your labours falling well short of your ideals and the resultant expense and irritation of having to do everything again.

This book is a result of my work as a landscaper/designer specialising for the last 14 years in water garden construction. My work has brought me face to face with all the problems presented by every style of water feature in every possible situation. Having dealt successfully with all these I found it disheartening to see people who could ill afford it attempting projects strewn with difficulties, many of which could have been solved long before the first sod of soil was shifted.

The easiest solution would have been to call in a landscaper to put the ideas into reality. However disproportionate labour costs, coupled with the fact that water-garden construction is a very labour intensive area of landscaping, can often make the simplest of projects inordinately expensive. I feel it is much better that everyone be provided with all the necessary information to build his or her own water garden. The creation of this self-sufficient world in your garden where constant growth and activity is a ceaseless reward to all the senses will be a source of never-ending pleasure and satisfaction.

To create the successful water garden is to provide a place in your garden where all the flora and fauna are totally interdependent. As the seasons pass by things flourish and die. Plants may get out of hand, there may be epidemics of algae or parasites or even huge populations of toads and tadpoles. Unless your pond is constructed employing the correct basic principles these events in a pond's life will be problems rather than the see-saw effect of nature's natural balance.

SITING

The first points to consider about the water garden are to do with siting. Check these points:

1. The pool should be in full sun. Nearly all plants associated with water, especially lilies, need some direct sunlight to flower.
2. The pool should be away from trees and where prevailing winds will not carry poisonous leaves into the pond. Smaller ponds can be netted against the worst of the autumn fall and a few leaves do not harm a healthy pond. However avoid Willow, Elder, Poplars, Laburnum, Yew and Oak.
3. Avoid too much exposure to north or prevailing winds.
4. Avoid the boggy, water-logged area at the bottom of the garden.
5. Consider accessibility to a water supply.
6. If there are to be waterfalls or fountains consider the distance from a power supply to connect a pump.
7. Consider children. Where there is water they will be in it, and at some point probably head-first!
8. Since we spend so much of the year looking at our gardens from inside our houses it is good to have a view of the water garden, or part of it, from the house.
9. Are there electricity lines, bedrock, pipework, or tanks where you choose to have your water garden?

PLANNING

Plan every sod of earth you dig and every trowel of cement you mix. Go through the job from start to finish in your mind working out quantities and costs.

Having chosen the site, choose the best shape. Pools closer to the house tend to be more formal. Lay a rope or hose on the ground to get the best idea. Then try to draw a plan of the pool in relation to the rest of the garden. Ideally sketch how you see it from where you are most often going to view it, or take a photograph of the site and draw the pool in position on a tracing of it.

SIZE AND SHAPE

Make the pond as large as your pocket or energy will allow. The larger they are the steadier is the balance they maintain. The absolute minimum size is 30 sq ft.

Unless you plan to keep Koi Carp a depth of more than 30in is unnecessary; 18-24in is adequate.

If you are using a liner, keep the shape as simple as possible as dramatic shapes use excess liner and create unsightly folds.

Beware of making a stream disproportionately large in relation to the pool. Remember, the stream needs an addition of at least half an inch of water added to its surface to get it flowing. Not only this; there is a backlog of water that seems to get hidden in the system. This can mean a considerable loss of water in the pool once the stream is in full flood. The marginal plants in particular cannot stand the radical rise and fall of waterlevels.

MATERIALS

Get your materials (liners, pumps etc) from a reliable retailer close at hand. As you look into what is available you find that the competitiveness of the industry has created a range of materials whose price is related to performance and durability. In other words you get what you pay for! Better quality products are highly recommended for more ambitious projects, even if it means having to cut back on the size.

With regard to pond construction, this book only covers the use of liners and preformed pools. General puddling is beyond the resources of most amateurs, and concrete ponds need considerable engineering and construction skills, not to mention time, patience and very deep pockets!

For further guidance on choice of materials see the list of facts and tips relating to individual items on page 6.

FILTERS, LIGHTS AND ELECTRICS

Items such as lighting and filters are not covered since their design and installation is constantly being updated. If they are to be included make allowance for them right from the initial planning stage. Detailed information about these can be obtained from your local supplier.

Very little is covered on the safe installation of electrical items. All these require a circuit breaker of the correct British Standard to be installed between lights and pumps in the garden and the domestic supply. If you are in any doubt about the current British Standards for the installation of a power supply in the garden consult an electrician.

All connections to this power supply should be made with the most modern waterproof connectors fitted with the utmost care.

HOW TO USE THIS BOOK

In choosing the style of water-garden you have in mind it would be advisable to browse through the rest of the pages in the book familiarising yourself with the style of presentation and the general principles employed. In so doing you can note the pages that are relevant to your project and use them as you would a recipe book. Each major project lists tools and materials, guiding you through the task and pointing out potential problems on the way. A guide for estimating quantities involved can be found on page 6.

THE EXCAVATION

Soil doubles in volume as it emerges from the ground. There is always more than you need for further landscaping. The average large skip holds 6 cubic metres.

BLOCKS

For lined pools in the ground double the length and breadth and divide by two thirds for the number of blocks. For raised pools divide the height out of the ground by 9in and multiply the perimeter number of blocks by this number. Allow extra blocks for the creation of the marginal shelf in raised pools and pools set in unstable ground. Blockwork for the lined streams and waterfalls differs from project to project, but a commonsense figure can be deduced from the "head" of the stream or waterfall added onto its length and then doubled.

THE LINER

Remember to add double the depth to the length and breadth for the size. Economically it is best to design the pool in one dimension to fit in with the standard widths of liner sizes.

If you have dramatic indentations in the pool shape measure round the contour to take in the extra liner that is required to accommodate this shape.

STONEWORK AND ROCKERIES

I always estimate the quantity of stone for a rockery by multiplying the height by the width in feet and taking each square foot as accounting for 1 cwt or 50kg. This is the same for estimating the rockery surround and the stream face.

- Stonewalling usually covers about 4 sq yd faced area per ton.
- Natural stone paving covers about 11 sq yd per ton.
- Gravel or gravel to dust for footings, 1 ton covers about 10 sq yd at 2in depth.
- Cement, allow 1 bag for every 4 of building sand.
- Sand for building. Allow 2 large bags for each 4 sq yd faced walling but more if there is a lot of back filling.
- Sand covers approximately 15 sq yd per ton at 2in on the base of the pool.
- Preformed slabs and bricks are usually sold and priced by the square yard or square metre.

CEMENT

All underwater cement surfaces must be treated with Silglaze, Pool Glaze or a similar product to prevent leaching of lime into the water of the pond. (In general a 4:1 sand cement mix is adequate with the correct amount of waterproofer added.)

PUMP AND PIPEWORK

Always go for the largest practical diameter hose. This allows the pump to perform at its most efficient, but for every 10ft in length of hose it will lose between 60 and 100 gallons per hour in power. The performance in pumping vertically (the head) varies considerably from one make of pump to another. Details are generally given on individual pump performances by manufacturers on their products' boxes. Go for more power than you think you will need. If you are running a fountain from a waterfall pump this will reduce its performance by at least 30%.

STREAMS AND WATERFALLS

A flow of 300 gallons per hour will pour over a 3in sill about half an inch deep; over a 6in sill about a quarter of an inch deep. Allow a flow rate of 50-60 gallons per hour per inch of sill.

To avoid plant disturbance do not turn over more than the volume of the pond every hour. (In other words, a 300 gallon pond should not have a waterfall churning out more than 300 gallons per hour.)

FILTERS

If a pool filter is desired, to perform adequately it must be capable of turning over half the volume of the pool per hour with the pump situated as far away from the filter as possible. Filters are more efficient at keeping water clear when there is an Ultraviolet sterilising unit incorporated into the system.

Biological filters need a month to become fully operational in a digesting capacity. Since they function with the aid of micro-organisms which depend upon oxygen, a continuous flow of water is essential. They must therefore be operating continuously. For this reason it is best to have the filter system as a separate entity from waterfalls or fountains.

PLANTS

For more details on plants, see pages 21 and 29. I stress that oxygenating plants, such as Elodea Crispa, are the most essential ingredient of the pond. The ultimate aim is to have the pond 60% full of oxygenators; otherwise you are nowhere near guaranteeing a perfectly balanced system and therefore perfectly clear water. One bunch for every 2 sq ft of surface area will set you off.

FISH

When estimating the number of fish, remember that they soon grow into bigger fish. Never introduce too many fish in one go and wait 2-3 weeks after planting. Allow only 2in of fish per square foot of surface area. Take care in introducing new fish to a pool. Float the bag on the surface of the pool for 15-30 minutes, gradually introducing small quantities of water from their future home. This takes the stress out of changes in temperature and alkalinity. Then the fish can very slowly be introduced to their new environment.

FINALLY

Since I have to order in a variety of units, I have mixed metric and imperial measures in this book. A conversion table is given.

Building water-gardens can be hard and strenuous work. Take it easy, then, mind your back, and try to get some help. By the way, good luck!

Having mapped and measured the potential area for your water garden at home you will be surprised that what seem enormous pools stacked up at the Garden Centre are quite small once installed in the ground.

Cost of Preformed?
Per sq ft they cost the same as liners with a similar guarantee.

Preformed Streams
These are much easier to install than a liner stream. But they are:
1. Difficult to install so that they look completely natural.

TIP: Stonework and peagravel laid in the units can disguise them to a large extent. It is effective apart from at the waterfall lips.

2. Preformed streams do have a tendency to move about, particularly after heavy rain or frost. This can be fixed easily provided that the movement has not created a spillage, resulting in the pond being completely emptied, so that the pump over-heats and burns out.

TIP: Instead of laying the units on sand use a lean 6:1 sand/cement dry mix on which to settle the units. Also backfill gaps in the rockery work around and below the unit. This will reduce the potential soil erosion.

Preformed Pools
On the face of it, preformed pools and streams seem to be the easy option when it comes to installation, but the DIY water-gardener may require the patience of a saint to get the plastic pond precisely level in situ.

A blockwork framework or a concrete collar is necessary to ensure that the preformed pool is perfectly level. This means you lose one of the advantages of choosing a preformed pool since you are having to start as though you were installing a liner. However there are enough tips on the following pages to keep the chances of getting it right first time firmly on your side.

Plastic or Fibreglass?
Plastic pools have a size limitation and present technology does not allow them to be moulded at more than the minimum recommended depth of 18in. Fibreglass is relatively expensive. Large pools must be thick enough to be self supporting with water in them.

SITING AND "FIRST DIG"

FOR INSTALLING THE PERFECT PREFORMED POOL

Decisions to make before you start
1. Siting (see page 5) and position.
2. Is the pool to be set in the ground, half in the ground, or how?
3. Is the site level? If not, is the pool to be rising out of the ground or is one end to be set in the ground (see page 14)?
4. If the site is level decide on the pool edging, eg rock edge, crazy paving or a mixture
5. If the pool is set in a lawn the paving needs to be set below or flush with the grass. Use a sample of the paving to gauge the depth of the top edge of the pool.
6. What are you going to do with the excavated soil? Make a rockery, for example?

Tools Checklist
Spade, mattock for heavy soils. Shovel, spirit level (longer the better), trowel, hose, barrow, lump hammer (if paving).

Materials Checklist
1. Sand for backfill support for the pool.
2. Sand for cement mortar.
3. Cement and lime.
4. Rock, paving or both.
5. If paving, half inch chippings to dust, or half inch chippings to sand, for footing.

Method
1. Having decided site and position, mark out shape of pool in situ using a spirit level and trowel, lime or sand as a marker.
2. Remove turf inside the marked area and put it aside.
3. Excavate the soil in the shape down to the same depths as the marginal shelf (generally about 9in).
4. Save the top soil.

Method

1. *Having excavated to the level of the marginal shelf, fit the pool in the hole.*

2. *Check the base is level and mark with a trowel the shape of the base in the hole. This is the guide for digging out the lower portion of the pool.*

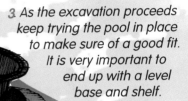

POOL

SOIL

3. *As the excavation proceeds keep trying the pool in place to make sure of a good fit. It is very important to end up with a level base and shelf.*

4. *Once you have the pool snugly fitting in the hole, the hole needs to be excavated a further inch to allow for a layer of sand in the base and on the shelves. This is also to ensure that the depth of any edging stones or paving may finish flush with the lawn.*

The earth from the excavation can be saved to form the basis of a waterfall or rockery. Be careful not to waste the first few inches of top soil by covering it with sub-soil as the digging out proceeds.

GRASS

EDGING PAVING STONE

POOL

MORTAR

LAYER OF SAND

Be careful not to overfill the pond.

Method

Using the remainder of the sand backfill between the pool and the surrounding soil. The most effective way is to wash the sand down the gap using the hose, whilst filling the pool with water. Great care must be taken to ensure that back wash between the pool and soil does not rise above the level of water in the pool.

2" FOOTING IS ENOUGH FOR ORDINARY HUMAN TRAFFIC.

If a path or formal edging is required remove the turf or soil around the edge of the pool to the required width and to the depth of the paving plus a footing.

Method

5mm of scalpings, or 2mm of chippings to dust, laid in a dry mix with cement (6:1) or compacted into the path area. This should finish level with the lip on the pool edge.

Rock Edge

Lay rocks on a good bed of mortar or cement with an inch overlap over the pool edge. If they are holding back soil ensure they knit together well and lean back slightly so that water and soil do not drain into the pool.

Cement

Pile of stones for wildlife exit to safety

Cement

Tube to carry cables

Ram

Falkaway from pond

Paving

Level

Mortar

Scalpings

Remember: If you want a pump or lights, lay a piece of tubing under the paving through which you can thread cables.

Crazy paving

1. *Lay out the pieces in position before fixing. Use the best pieces for edging the pool. Then place out the stones for the outside edge of the path. Use the rest of the material to fill in the centre.*

2. *Lay the pieces one by one on a bed of motar (cement, lime and sand in the ratio 1:1:6). Lay them level as you go round the pool and falling away slightly as you come away from the pool edge.*

Paving Slabs

Place the slabs in position. Where there is an odd number of slabs on one side, cut the centre slab in two and move the outside edges in to fit. Where an even number of slabs are required, cut the inside edge of the slabs at either end and move them in to fit flush.

TIP: start with one of the thickest pieces (this will "gauge" the mortar thickness required).

3. *Joint the pieces with fairly dry mortar, taking care to keep it off the paving pieces.*

Decide

1. Where the waterfalls will enter the pool. It looks best arriving at the most "curved out" part of the pool.

2. What shapes will you use? Always have a header pool at the top. This guarantees the falls having an even flow.

Pool

1" SAND

Bed the preformed waterfalls on an inch of sand in the excavation

Method

1. Excavate into the bank as exactly as possible the precise shape of the waterfalls. Start from the bottom. Also dig in the hose. The hose should travel through the soil by the shortest possible route.

MAKE SURE THE OUTLETS ARE LEVEL

2. The hose should be the maximum possible size for the pump.

The Pump

The flow rate of pumps is described in gallons per hour (gph) or litres per minute (lpm) or hour (lph). Estimate 50-60 gph for every inch of waterfall sill or 225-270 lph.

Rockery stone is placed in front of and around the top of the unit. The aim is to blend the units into the rockery. Putting peagravel into the bottom of units also helps. The point at which the hose enters the pool can be disguised by a planted basket of marginal plants.

Be prepared for movement as the soil settles over a period of time.

At the outlet into the top waterfall the hose can be hidden by flat stones placed upright in the units. Any exposed fibreglass or plastic will weather more quickly if roughened with glass-paper.

PREFORMED POOL

RAISED: EITHER FORMAL OR INFORMAL SHAPE

The alternative of having a raised pool or partially raised pool gives a variety of possible basic designs. These are of course more expensive and time consuming to build.

Materials: Chippings to dust (20mm) or chippings and sand, sand and cement, brick or building stone, slabs or crazy paving, blocks, junction box (electrical), pump, armoured cable.

Tools: Shovel, lump hammer, level, trowels, cold chisel, spade

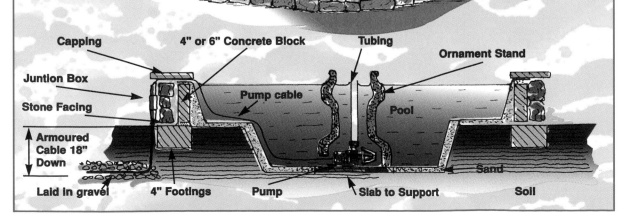

Capping

Juntion Box

Stone Facing

Armoured Cable 18" Down

Laid in gravel

4" Footings

4" or 6" Concrete Block

Pump cable

Pump

Tubing

Ornament Stand

Pool

Slab to Support

Sand

Soil

1. Mark an exact line around the edge of the pool in situ using a spirit level or plumbline.

2. Dig a trench round the pool 12in wide and 4in deep, using the mark as a guide. Take it under the pool the same width as the pool rim.

3. Hammer in pegs level with each other as a guide to level out concrete for footings.

Materials: Sand, cement, chippings, stone or brick. Slabs or paving.

4. Lay 4in concrete blocks under the rim of the pool. On the top row of blocks that support the rim leave 2in wide gaps between them. You will use these to feed the backfill of sand as the stone cladding is built up.

5. The pool is set on an inch of sand. Place some blocks for added support under the marginal shelf.

6. If a pump for a fountain is required do not forget to lay down a piece of piping which will later be bricked over. Thread a piece of cable through the pipe by which you can pull through the pump cable when necessary.

Tools: Spade, shovel, level, trowel, pegs, lump hammer

7. Lay building stone. Random stone: use larger stones around the base. Make sure the stones knit together as much as possible. Capping stones should all be positioned before they are laid.

This sort of feature is best set up against a strong reinforced wall so that it does not look like a small volcano (tump) and also to avoid excessive use of stone.

The most effective method of landscaping a stream is to set it in a cleft in an existing bank with the strata of the rock showing as the waterfall disappears right and left into the grass of the bank.

Both stream and rockery should appear to be of solid construction, so more stone is better than less.

Using the cut and fill method, lay the rock with the strata as horizontal as possible, except in the stream, where it can appear to have been altered by natural forces.

Individual rockery stones must be set leaning slightly backwards, so that rainwater drains back into the rockery.

Decide

1. Site and aspect and details of design.

2. Are you going to face the inside of the pool with rockery stone, building stone, both or nothing?

Method

1. Lay down a rope or hose-pipe to mark the pool shape.

2. Cut and remove the turf.

3. Dig out the first 9in down from the required level of the water. This will be the level of the marginal shelf.

Tools: Spade, shovel, level, straight edge, 2ft (60cm) pegs, trowel, lump hammer.

Materials: Sand, cement, pool liner, edging stone, 4in concrete blocks

4. Dig down a further 10in, leaving a ledge in the required places around the edge. Better to have more marginal shelf than you think is necessary. The width of the marginal shelf should be 12in plus the width of a 4in concrete block plus the width of any stone facing the inside of the liner - account for this when sizing up the liner.

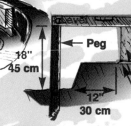

5. If soil from the second dig looks like lifeless sub-soil make sure it is kept separate from the top soil.

6. Using pegs marked for the required depth of pool, bang them in around the pool so that they are level and dig down to the marks. If there is going to be a paved pool surround then the proposed water level should be the thickness of the paving below the turf or soil.

7. The concrete blocks are laid on the marginal shelf level with the pegs to form the skeleton of the pond. Once laid on a normal 3:1 cement mix they will define the final water level.

8 When the blocks have set, dig out a footing for any paving. The depth will depend on the amount of traffic, human or otherwise, that is expected.

1. Excavate a trench at least 6in deep and 10in wide, the middle of which will be the circumference of the pool.

2. Bang level pegs in a little deeper than the depth of the surround slabs of the proposed pool.

Turf

Level Peg

3. Place shuttering in the trench at a 20 degree angle. "Lawn Edging" is ideal.

Shuttering

4. Pour concrete in the "land" side and temporarily back fill with soil on the "pool" side.

Soil Backfill

Concrete

5. Complete the pool excavation leaving a marginal shelf and remove the shuttering.

6. The liner can be folded into place as with the other methods. Paving and rockery stones can be cemented into place on the liner flap. These should end up laid just below the level of the lawn.

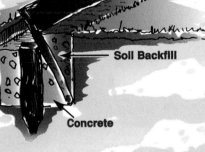

Slabs

Liner with sand and underlay

Soil

Method

1. Cut out and lay footing for the paving and lay a 6:3:2 concrete mix at least 2in (5cm) deep with a fall away from the pool.

2. Lay a protective 1in deep layer of sand on the bottom of the pool. Cover the blocks and hard edges with underlay or damp newspapers.

Tip: Trowl the sand flat with a plasters float.

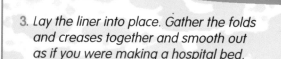

Underlay

Fall

Sand

3. Lay the liner into place. Gather the folds and creases together and smooth out as if you were making a hospital bed.

4. Cut the liner shape allowing a generous overlap of at least 6in over the blocks.

Tip: for pools with radical scallops, measure the width around the contour of the shape as this will take up extra liner.

Money saving tip: Build your pond to a size that, at least in one direction, corresponds to a "standard" width in the material you choose.

Warning: Awkward Shapes make for extra folds.

Remember: Calculate the liner size by adding twice the maximum pool depth to both the length and width of pool. Take care to measure overall pond dimensions (ie, at the widest points).

Tip: Drape a tape measure through the excavation to check you have the right size - before you unpack the liner.

DRESSING THE INSIDE OF THE POOL

WITH WALLING OR ROCKERY STONE

To give the appearance that the pool is constructed from solid stone by dressing the inside of the pool down to the level of the marginal shelf, either with a wall or rockery stone.

A rockery can be made to appear as though it continues right down into the water

If you intend to stabilize the rockery or walling by cementing use waterproofing liquid or powder in the mix.

1. In the construction of the pool leading up to the fitting of the liner it is necessary to allow for the average width of the stone in gauging how wide the marginal shelf should be.

Dress gaps with gravel or peagravel.

FALL

Underlay under stones

oncrete
lock

Width of walling

Width of large plant basket

Liner

Underlay

Width of large plant basket

4" concrete block

Width of rockery stone

2. In the initial planning of the pool, the width of "materials laid" (ie, walling stone, brick or rockery) must be added to the liner size when ordering, plus twice the depth, in order to end up with the required size of the pool.

Here flat bottomed rockery stone sits on the marginal shelf and is built up to or just below the water level of the pond, forming a trough lined with underlay which provides the marginal planting area.

A rock facing forms a planting trough for marginals.

"Gravel" dressing

Water level

Liner

Chemical free soil

4" concrete block

Brick facing to the upper side of the pool from the marginal shelf level. This can be brick or stone laid using a cement mix with a water-proofing additive.

Underlay under stones to protect liner

Underlay under liner and to line planting trough

Brick to disguise the liner and make a very high water level

Beware: Large quantities of cement exposed to the water need to be treated with Silglase or a similar product to prevent leaching of lime into the water.

Water level

Marginal shelf

Water proof pointing

Liner PVC, butyl or rubber

This product is painted onto the cement that is going to be under water and then washed off. This is done in prescribed amounts and rinsed off after certain intervals. Follow the manufacturer's instructions.

4" concrete block

underlay

CONSERVATIONIST'S DREAM

The pond is created using the basic techniques, but a hump is left on the inside edge of the marginal shelf. Underlay is laid on top of and below the liner in order to protect it.

If possible keep liner turned up above water level to help prevent leaching or siphoning by capillary action.

WHITE LILY OR YELLOW NUPHAR LUTEA

Liner

Soil

Underlay

Hump on marginal shelf to retain soil in pool margin.

Soil (a rough sandy sub-soil is best) is laid on top of this, smoothing out the levels cut by the excavation to dish with gently sloping sides. This creates a natural look and easy access is created for wildlife.

Beware: Do not make the inclines so steep that the soil will all slip down into the base of the pool.

Some native marginals:
Acorus calamus (Sweet Flag)
Butomus umbellatus (Flowering Rush)
Caltha Palustris (Kingcup)
Iris Pseudocorus (Yellow Flag)
Lysimachia Nummularia (Creeping Jenny)
Lythrum Salicaria (Loosestrife)
Sagittaria Sagittifolia (Arrowhead)
Veronica Baccabunga

Bear in mind:
Even the most balanced pond or pool eventually needs to be cleaned out. This means all that mud will have to come out and plants, which will have grown into massive clumps, will have to be thinned.

Alternative
German Method

Slab or kerb edging

Soil

Dispensing with soil in the bottom. Lilies etc can still be planted in containers or hessian bags.

Footing or block

If the soil is not particularly firm or "clayey" (argillaceous) then this hump could be created out of a fillet of cement or concrete.

Liner

Underlay

Dig out the waterway from the spoil heap or bank next to the pond for steep waterfalls.

<u>*Water level:*</u> *remember when the water is flowing the level can rise by an inch in the ponds and over the outlet shelf.*

Stream

Pool liner

4" or 6" concrete blocks

Sand   **Liner**

TIPS. Work up from the bottom, that is the water level of the pond. Do not get ambitious: streams work out very expensive.

In theory the watercourse can be lined with pieces of liner overlapping. However you do use a lot less and it is "fail safe" to use one piece draping right into the pond.

1. Divide it into a series of pools, one dropping into another. Make sure the soil is well compacted (see below). Allow space for a skeleton of concrete blocks to be laid that will define the watercourse. At each level the blocks must be laid level (see below) apart from an outlet at least 4in below the block level for the water to flow to the next level.

Beware:
If this slope is created from the spoil of the pond there is bound to be a certain drop in level unless it has been consolidating for 18 months. Soil doubles in volume on excavation.

Brick or half blocks

Therefore:
1. Consolidate the soil as much as possible.

Sand

Hose should be as large as the proposed pump can take.

2. After cement is dry backfill behind the blocks.

3. A 1in layer of sand can be laid throughout the stream underlay over blocks.

Pool **Blocks**

Make sure the face of the waterfall is well back behind the end of the side blocks at that level.

4. Lay the hose for the pump along the most sensible route. Excavate a trench for it but do not backfill until you start to build the rockery.

2. When constructing the waterfall framework, tilt each unit towards the outlet, ie build each pool higher at the back,
or Build the blockwork up from solid unworked ground or footings.

WITH LINERS

1. Mark out the course of the stream, bearing in mind the performance of the pump you intend to use. One inch of sill per 50-60 gallons plus width of stone.

Level

Level

6ft

2. If you are using heavy stone dig out the stream, making it 8in wider and 4in deeper than is needed. The fall must be at least 1 in 80. Start from the bottom and finish with a header pool. That will help to steady the flow from the pump.

3. Using 4in concrete blocks and a 3:1 sand/cement mix define the sides of the stream. Follow the contour of the slope if it is gentle. If it becomes steeper step it down (see page 22). The sides must be level with each other.

4. When the cement is dry backfill behind the blocks with soil.

5. For every 4in drop, a level of bricks or a "frog" of cement must dam the causeway at the same level as the base of the previous row of bricks. Therefore Point A is the same level as Aa and B the same as Bb etc. This ensures that a water level is maintained throughout the stream.

Aa

A

B

Stones for base of stream.

Bb

6. Line the stream with sand and underlay over the blockwork. The water stays above the stones in the bottom of the steam obscuring the liner.

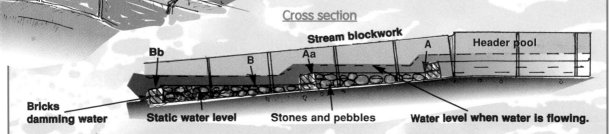

Cross section

Stream blockwork

Bb

B

Aa

A

Header pool

Bricks damming water　　**Static water level**　　**Stones and pebbles**　　**Water level when water is flowing.**

Estimate the stream liner length as length on the horizontal plus twice the height. Width is dictated by the width of the liner strips. Liner 5ft wide produces 2ft to 2ft 6in header pools with 9in to 12in outlets. Liner 10ft wide produces 4ft to 6ft headers with 2ft outlets.

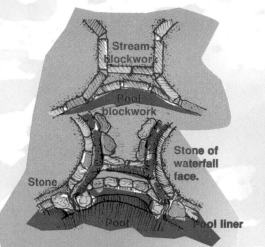

Stream blockwork

Pool blockwork

Stone of waterfall face.

Stone

Pool

Pool liner

Final fall
Birds eye view of structure

TIP: If you want to cut down on the use of cement within the stream, bedding stones down into a thick bed of peagravel is possible. It also makes for easy repair work in the future and acts as a rudimentary filter.

1. Lay underlay over the blockwork.

2. Lay the liner in place with a large overlap right into the pool.

3. Carefully push and fold the liner into place, gathering as many creases as possible together and making sure the liner fits into the contours of the blockwork.

4. Thoughtfully trim off some of the excess liner.

5. Line the stream with stonework.

TIP. Stone laid straight onto liner can be cushioned with offcuts of underlay.

TIPS:(a) Start from the bottom of the stream and work up.
(b) Concentrate on the face of each waterfall and work outwards into the rockery or wall retaining the earth.
(c) Always think in terms of retaining the water in the stream within the liner. You are just putting a facing on the liner.
(d) Tuck stream liner up between side facing stones to prevent water travelling sideways.

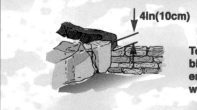

↓ 4in(10cm)

Top of wall level with outlet block- work allowing enough room to be capped with slab or slate.

See (d) left

WATERFALL FACING TECHNIQUES

FORMAL OR MIRROR WATERFALLS

1.

2.

Fall →

Groove

Pool liner

Stream liner

3.

4.

**Basic Informal Fall
Simple Japanese Pattern**

TIPS.
1. Place the stones in order of letters.
2. Backfill behind the stones with cement, making sure the liner flaps stand out to prevent sideways seepage.

(A) Mirror stone
(B&C) Flanking stones
(D&E) Base stones
(F) Water dividing stone
(G) Wave dividing stone
(H) Header stone

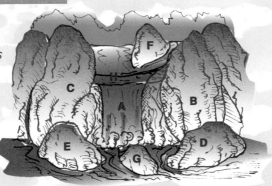

"White" water boulder cascade.

Japanese Ribbon Waterfall

Footing required

The Child Safe Pebble Pool

1. Excavate a hole 3ft or 1 metre in diameter. Lay in a framework of 4in concrete blocks.

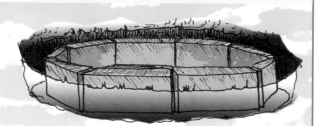

2. The blocks are covered with underlay and then liner material.

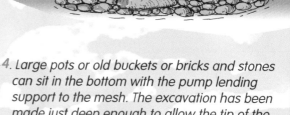

3. A grill of galvanised steel mesh or rigid plastic netting is held in place with hooks or masonry nails. This will support the layer of cobbles.

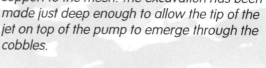

4. Large pots or old buckets or bricks and stones can sit in the bottom with the pump lending support to the mesh. The excavation has been made just deep enough to allow the tip of the jet on top of the pump to emerge through the cobbles.

A Bubbling Boulder

Plants are planted in groups in the surrounding gravel. Boulders can be purchased ready drilled. See your local stone merchant.

An Everflowing Grecian Urn

The hose into the urn is held and sealed into place with silicone, mastic or plasticine.

A Watering Watering-can.

The main problem and probably the most expensive aspect of this sort of feature can be getting the power to it.

DESIGN FOR A FORMAL POOL

LINED WITH PVC SET IN A PATIO OF YORKSTONE PAVING SLABS *15ft long x 7 ft 6in wide x 18 in deep.*

In planning:

Work to standard liner widths.

1. *Dig hole to correct size plus 10in to allow room for the concrete blocks.*

2. *Lay 4in x 18in x 9in concrete blocks on a 4in footing (see "raised preformed pool" page 14).*

3. *An inside row of concrete blocks is laid and backfilled with 6:1 concrete mix to form a marginal shelf.*

4. *2in of sand is laid in the bottom.*

5. *Underlay to be laid over blocks.*

> TIP: Build the pond to the size 15ft x 7ft 6in measured from the internal face of the blocks. The exact size should be determined by the size of the edging slabs, bearing in mind that it is best to have a 1in overhang of slabs over the pool, so that if the slabs were exactly 18in including the pointing then the pool internal diameter should be 15ft 2in x 7ft 8in.

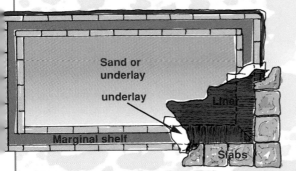

Sand or underlay

underlay

Liner

Marginal shelf

Slabs

Front edge of pool may be above lawn level. In this case face it with suitable stone or brick.

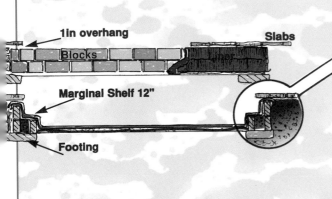

1in overhang

Blocks

Slabs

Liner

Marginal Shelf 12"

Footing

Liner

Block

Marginal shelf

Block

Backfill

Block

Block

Footing

Sand

Backfill lean - Mix 6:1 cement chippings to dust.

6. *Liner 20ft x 11ft is loosely laid and folded into position. Tuck liner behind blocks before backfilling.*

7. *Lay the slabs on top of the liner using backfill as a footing.*

Alternative

Stone facing obscuring the first 10" of liner. For this method the concrete block framework must be built allowing for the width of this and double the width of the stonework must be added to the length and breadth of the liner.

Although these features fit in perfectly with general principles employed in this book, it is imperative that if they are required they be incorporated in the plan right from the start - especially the beach.

Beach

Bog Garden

Stepping Stones

Jetty

Jetty

Pressure treated timber

Pool frame work blocks

Liner wrapping

Beach

Set slightly below water level

Stepping Stones

Pebbles

Pool

Underlay on pool liner

Sandy infill

Underlay

Liner

A box of 4" x 9" x 18" concrete blocks filled with concrete can be sealed with G4 (a moisture-cured polyurethane which forms a non-porous seal).

Edging stone

Marginal shelf

Edging stone

Bog garden

Pool

Marginal shelf

Aquatic soil or chemical free soil

Bog garden liner with holes spiked through all over

1½" Pipe to take water to the roots

Soil with leaf mould and coarse sand

Clean rubble

Drainage holes in the liner

Up turned turves

18"

PLANTS

THE ESSENTIAL INGREDIENTS

A pool or pond cannot survive as a self-sufficient world without plants.
Most of the wildlife, apart from fish, will make their own way to a new pool.

The lead strips used by retailers for tying bunches together do not contaminate.

For pool cover and focal point

2. Lilies and deep water aquatics. Allow one lily for every 25 sq ft.

For algae control and pool cover

3. Floating plants. They use up the mineral resources that algae consume. Allow 1 for every 10 sq ft.

Beware: Many marginal plants spread and take over very rapidly. Cheap lilies are vigorous. Do homework on species and varieties. In small ponds plant mixed baskets with varieties of leaf shape colour and height.

For softening the pool edge and using up mineral resources

4. Marginal plants. Allow 1 marginal for every 5 sq ft.

Most water plant containers need liners (hessian or coco fibre). Fill with chemical free soil.

Top off with peagravel

Most important
1. Oxygenating plants. Elodea crispa (Lagarosiphon Major) is one of the best. Potamageton crispus (Curly pondweed) or Water Crowsfoot for streams. Just push bunches of 4 or 5 strands into baskets of peagravel, 25 to 50 bunches per basket, allowing one bunch for every 2 sq ft of surface area.

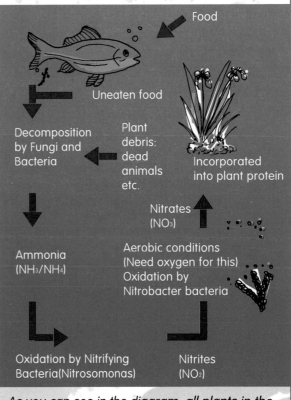

Food

Uneaten food

Decomposition by Fungi and Bacteria

Plant debris: dead animals etc.

Incorporated into plant protein

Nitrates (NO_3)

Ammonia (NH_3/NH_4)

Aerobic conditions (Need oxygen for this) Oxidation by Nitrobacter bacteria

Oxidation by Nitrifying Bacteria (Nitrosomonas)

Nitrites (NO_2)

As you can see in the diagram, all plants in the pond form an essential link in the ecosystem. Most importantly, the oxygenating plants or pond weeds help to provide the oxygen necessary to convert nitrites to nitrates. If the plant life fails to maintain the link in the chain, the pool becomes stagnant.

18"-2ft

Floating plants

9"-1ft

Lily   **Oxygenators**   **Deep water marginal**   **Marginals at water level**

Induction Drive Pumps

Easy to maintain, cheap to run, well-designed induction drive pumps with centrifugal rotor design give years of trouble free running.

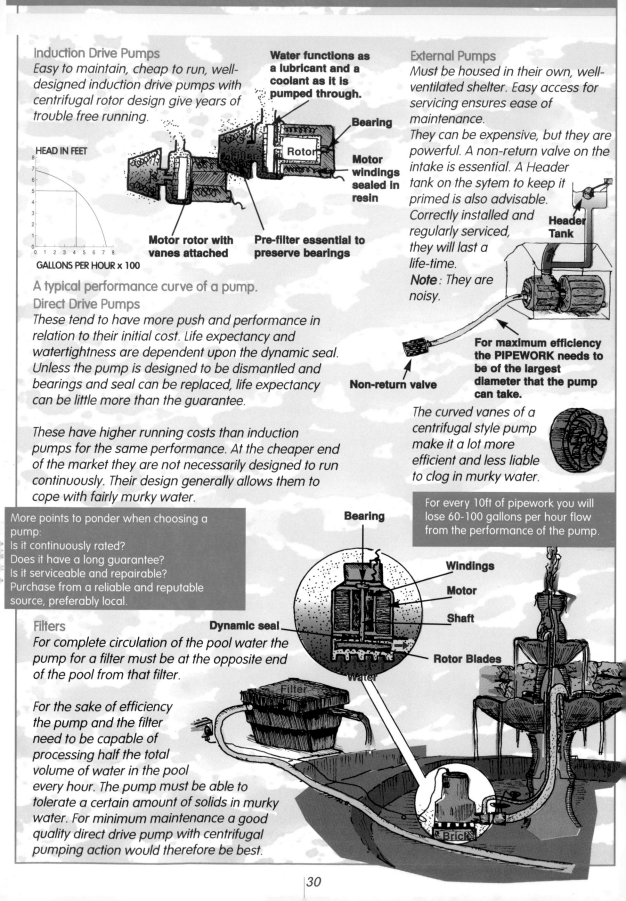

Water functions as a lubricant and a coolant as it is pumped through.

Bearing

Rotor

Motor windings sealed in resin

HEAD IN FEET

GALLONS PER HOUR x 100

Motor rotor with vanes attached

Pre-filter essential to preserve bearings

A typical performance curve of a pump.

Direct Drive Pumps

These tend to have more push and performance in relation to their initial cost. Life expectancy and watertightness are dependent upon the dynamic seal. Unless the pump is designed to be dismantled and bearings and seal can be replaced, life expectancy can be little more than the guarantee.

These have higher running costs than induction pumps for the same performance. At the cheaper end of the market they are not necessarily designed to run continuously. Their design generally allows them to cope with fairly murky water.

More points to ponder when choosing a pump:
Is it continuously rated?
Does it have a long guarantee?
Is it serviceable and repairable?
Purchase from a reliable and reputable source, preferably local.

Filters

For complete circulation of the pool water the pump for a filter must be at the opposite end of the pool from that filter.

For the sake of efficiency the pump and the filter need to be capable of processing half the total volume of water in the pool every hour. The pump must be able to tolerate a certain amount of solids in murky water. For minimum maintenance a good quality direct drive pump with centrifugal pumping action would therefore be best.

External Pumps

Must be housed in their own, well-ventilated shelter. Easy access for servicing ensures ease of maintenance.

They can be expensive, but they are powerful. A non-return valve on the intake is essential. A Header tank on the sytem to keep it primed is also advisable. Correctly installed and regularly serviced, they will last a life-time.

Note: *They are noisy.*

Header Tank

Non-return valve

For maximum efficiency the PIPEWORK needs to be of the largest diameter that the pump can take.

The curved vanes of a centrifugal style pump make it a lot more efficient and less liable to clog in murky water.

For every 10ft of pipework you will lose 60-100 gallons per hour flow from the performance of the pump.

Bearing

Windings

Motor

Shaft

Dynamic seal

Rotor Blades

Water

Filter

Brick

the perfect
POND
recipe book

CONVERSION TABLES

Length:

1 inch = 25.4 millimetres	1 millimetre = 0.0394 inches
1 inch = 2.54 centimetres	1 centimetre = 0.394 inches
1 foot = 30.5 centimetres	1 metre = 39.4 inches
1 foot = 0.305 metres	1 metre = 3.28 feet
1 yard = 0.914 metres	1metre = 1.09 yards
1 mile = 0.609 kilometres	1 kilometre = 0.621 miles

Weight:

1 ounce = 28.3 grams	1 gram = 0.035 ounce
1 pound = 454 grams	1 kilogram = 2.2 pounds
1 pound = 0.454 kilograms	1 metric tonne = 2200 pounds
1 ton = 1.02 metric tonnes	1 metric tonne = 0.984 tons

Capacity:

1 fluid ounce = 28.4 millilitres	1 millilitres = 0.035 fluid ounces
1 pint = 0.568 litres	1 litre = 1.76 pints
1 UK gallon = 4.55 litres	1 litre = 0.22 UK gallons
1 UK gallon = 1.2 US gallons	1 US gallon = 0.833 UK gallons

Area:

1 sq inch = 6.45 sq centimetres	1 sq centimetre = 0.155 sq inches
1 sq foot = 929 sq centimetres	1 sq metre = 10.76 sq feet
1 sq foot = 0.093 sq metres	1 sq metre = 1.2 sq yard
1 sq yard = 0.836 sq metres	1 hectare = 2.47 acres
1 acre = 0.405 hectares	1 sq kilometre = 247 acres
1 sq mile = 259 hectares	1 sq kilometre = 0.386 sq miles
1 sq mile = 2.59 sq kilometres	

Volume:

1 cu inch = 16.4 cu centimetres	1 cu centimetre = 0.061 cu inches
1 cu foot = 0.028 cu metres	1 cu metre = 35.3 cu feet
1 cu yard = 0.765 cu metres	1 cu metre = 1.31 cu yards

Abbreviations:

centimetre(s): ....cm
foot, feet: ....ft
gram(s): ....g
inch(es): ....in, "
kilogram(s): ....kg
metre(s): ....m
millimetre(s): ....mm
ounce(s): ....oz
pound(s): ....lb